LITTLE LIBRARY

Flags

Philip Steele

Kingfisher

NEW YORK

Contents

All kinds of flags

Flags can be seen almost everywhere. They flutter and flap from the tops of important buildings, from flagpoles at ceremonies and games, and from ships at sea. Some flags are used as bright, cheerful decorations on objects such as T-shirts and mugs. Others are used as warnings and signals.

Shapes and designs

F lags come in all shapes, sizes, and colors. They may be made of cloth, paper, or even plastic. Today, most flags are rectangular in shape, but there are many other flag designs. Some of these are shown below.

A pennant or streamer has a long tail.

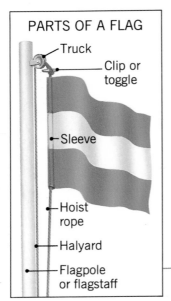

PARTS OF A FLAG

- Truck
- Clip or toggle
- Sleeve
- Hoist rope
- Halyard
- Flagpole or flagstaff

Swallowtail flags have V-shaped cuts in their outer edges.

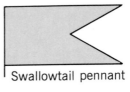

Swallowtail pennant

Swallowtail with tongue

Bunting is a string of flags.

COLLECTING FLAGS

Why don't you start a collection of flags or things with flag designs on them? Stamps, clothes, badges, mugs, and plates are often decorated with flags.

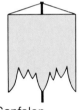

Gonfalon
(hanging banner)

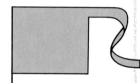

Schwenkel (square or rectangular with a tail)

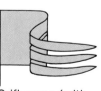

Oriflamme (with streamers)

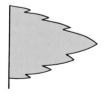

Oriental with flammules (flame-shaped cuts)

The first flags

T housands of years ago, people may have placed animal skulls or horns on poles as badges of their tribe. Warriors probably carried symbols of their gods into battle for good luck. Armies of the ancient Romans carried standards that they thought were holy. The Roman vexillum was one of the first flags in Europe.

These standards are called vexilloids. They were probably used to show where the chief was during a battle or to signal the movement of troops.

Bronze and silver standard (about 2300 B.C.)

Egyptian vexilloid (about 3200 B.C.)

ROMAN STANDARDS

Eagle standard of a Roman legion

Vexillum – an early kind of flag

Standard of the Emperor Constantine

THE FLYING DRAGON

During the Middle Ages, soldiers carried dragon flags into battle to frighten the enemy. These flags were shaped like wind socks and contained whistles that shrieked when the wind blew through them.

Coats of arms

W hen battles were fought by knights in armor, it was hard to see which side people belonged to. About 900 years ago in Europe, family badges called coats of arms were designed for kings, queens, and knights. These coats of arms were sewn or painted on clothes, shields, and flags. The set of rules for designing these shields was called heraldry.

Heraldic shields were divided into simple patterns. Many of today's national flags use similar designs.

Japanese knights tied flags to their backs so that they could be seen in battle.

Modern city flags often show an old coat of arms, like this flag from Amsterdam in Holland.

YOUR OWN FLAG

1 Sketch out a flag design on a sheet of paper. You could base the design on your initials, or you could draw something to do with your surname (such as a crown if your name is King).

2 Copy the design onto an old sheet and color it in with fabric paints or felt-tip markers.

3 Finally, cut out the sheet into the shape of a flag.

Flags at sea

I n the past, many ships flew flags showing their country's or city's coat of arms. Most of these were hard to see from a distance and so simpler flags were designed, with bold crosses or stripes. Later, many of these flags became national flags.

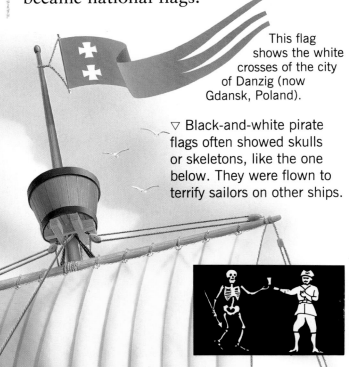

This flag shows the white crosses of the city of Danzig (now Gdansk, Poland).

▽ Black-and-white pirate flags often showed skulls or skeletons, like the one below. They were flown to terrify sailors on other ships.

SIGNALS AT SEA

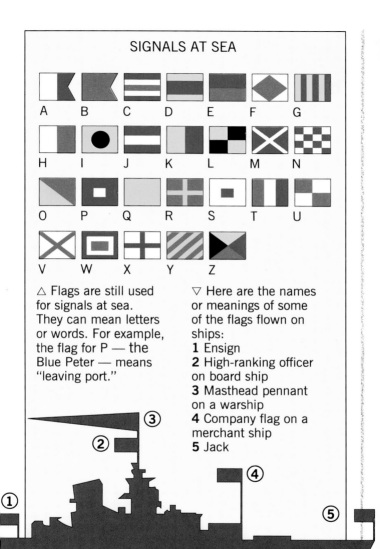

A B C D E F G

H I J K L M N

O P Q R S T U

V W X Y Z

△ Flags are still used for signals at sea. They can mean letters or words. For example, the flag for P — the Blue Peter — means "leaving port."

▽ Here are the names or meanings of some of the flags flown on ships:
1 Ensign
2 High-ranking officer on board ship
3 Masthead pennant on a warship
4 Company flag on a merchant ship
5 Jack

Flags on land

Many companies have their own flags. These flags may show advertising slogans or carry company badges called logos. The one shown below left, for example, is the logo for a car-maker. Special organizations may also have their own flags.

World Scout organization

Red Crescent organization

Company logo (for Volks-wagen)

Red Cross organization

Crosses and crescents, like the ones shown above right, are religious symbols. They appear on many national flags, too. Religious flags are often carried in processions.

Buddhist flag

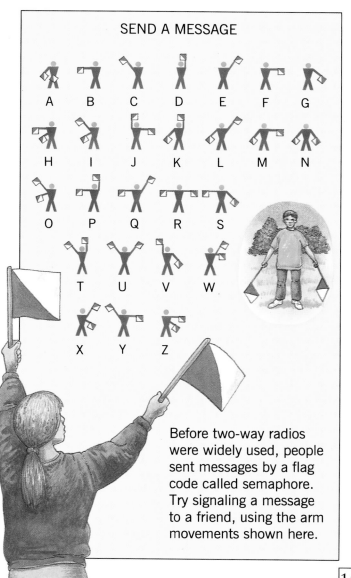

SEND A MESSAGE

A B C D E F G

H I J K L M N

O P Q R S

T U V W

X Y Z

Before two-way radios were widely used, people sent messages by a flag code called semaphore. Try signaling a message to a friend, using the arm movements shown here.

Sporting flags

$\mathbf{A}$t big sporting events, fans often wave flags and banners in their team's colors. National and local teams all have their own flags. Small flags are often used as markers in games such as golf, and as signals in horse racing, yachting, and football.

▽ A checkered flag signals the end of a car race.

▷ Small flags are used to mark the corners on soccer fields.

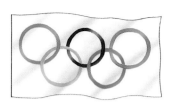

The five colored rings on the Olympic flag represent the world's five continents. Every Olympic Games also has its own special flag.

Flag ceremonies

M any people have deep feelings about flags. Flags may stand for strongly held beliefs or be part of a country's history. They may represent peace or freedom. Many countries have special ceremonies in which soldiers or school children salute their flag as a sign of respect.

At the Palio festival in Siena, Italy, colorful historic flags are tossed and swirled in the air.

FLAG FACTS

● When important people die, flags may be lowered part way — flown at half-mast — as a sign of respect.

● Lowering a flag or flying it upside down may be seen as a sign of surrender.

● Ships sometimes salute each other by dipping their flags — lowering and raising them slightly as they pass each other.

National flags may be flown outside palaces and other important buildings. Many are raised or lowered daily by a special guard of honor.

Flag ceremony in Morocco

National flags

Today, every country in the world has its own national flag. On the next pages, you can see a selection of these flags. National flags are often flown side by side as a mark of friendship between countries.

National flags may be flown to show respect to a visiting king, queen, or president.

INTERNATIONAL FLAGS

Some flags are well-known throughout the world. Perhaps the most famous is that of the United Nations which shows two olive branches to represent world peace.

United Nations

European Community

Organization of
American States

Organization of
African Unity

Africa

Morocco

Algeria

Mauritania

Gambia

Guinea

Sierra Leone

Liberia

Côte d'Ivoire

Mali

Burkina Faso

Ghana

Benin

Nigeria

Niger

Chad

Libya

Egypt

Sudan

Ethiopia

Djibouti

Somalia

Cameroon

Mozambique

Kenya

Gabon

Zimbabwe

Uganda

Congo

Botswana

Tanzania

Angola

Namibia

Rwanda

Zambia

South Africa

Zaire

Malawi

Lesotho

Swaziland

Asia

Kazakhstan

Turkmenistan

Uzbekistan

Tajikistan

Kyrgyzstan

Turkey

Cyprus

Lebanon

Israel

Jordan

Saudi Arabia

Yemen

United Arab
Emirates

Bahrain

Kuwait

Iraq

Iran

Afghanistan

Pakistan

India

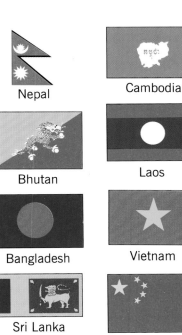
Nepal

Cambodia

Japan

Bhutan

Laos

Taiwan

Bangladesh

Vietnam

Philippines

Sri Lanka

China

Brunei

Maldives

Mongolia

Malaysia

Myanmar

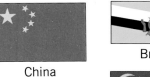
Korea, North

Singapore

Thailand

Korea, South

Indonesia

25

Europe

United Kingdom

Italy

Iceland

Netherlands

Vatican City State

Norway

Belgium

Switzerland

Sweden

Luxembourg

Austria

Finland

France

Germany

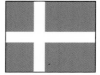
Denmark

Spain

Ireland

Portugal

Poland

Czech Republic

Slovakia

Hungary

Bosnia-
Herzegovina

Croatia

Yugoslavia
(Serbia and Montenegro)

Slovenia

Albania

Greece

Romania

Russia

Estonia

Latvia

Lithuania

Belarus

Ukraine

Moldova

Georgia

Armenia

Azerbaijan

North and Central America

Canada

United States

Mexico

Guatemala

Belize

El Salvador

Honduras

Nicaragua

Costa Rica

Panama

Bahamas

Cuba

Jamaica

Haiti

Dominican Republic

Dominica

Barbados

Grenada

Trinidad & Tobago

South America

Venezuela

Colombia

Paraguay

Guyana

Ecuador

Uruguay

Surinam

Peru

Chile

Brazil

Bolivia

Argentina

Oceania

Papua New Guinea

New Zealand

Tuvalu

Australia

Kiribati

Tonga

29

Index